Letters to my Son

MAVEN PRESS

Copyright © Laura Elizabeth
First published in Australia in 2022
by Maven Press
Roleystone WA 6111

Cover Design by Kristy Jamieson
Edited by Jade Bell

All rights reserved. No part of this book may be used or reproduced by any means, graphic, electronic, or mechanical, including photocopying, recording, taping or by any information storage retrieval system without the written permission of the copyright owner except in the case of brief quotations embodied in critical articles and reviews.

Because of the dynamic nature of the Internet, any web addresses or links contained in this book may have changed since publication and may no longer be vaild. The views expressed in this work are solely those of the author and do not necessarily reflect the views of the publisher and the publisher hereby disclaims any responsibility for them.

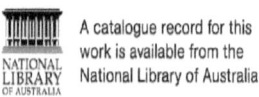

A catalogue record for this work is available from the National Library of Australia

National Library of Australia Catalogue-in-Publication data:
Letters to my Son/Laura Elizabeth

ISBN: 978-0-6453230-8-5
(Paperback)
ISBN: 978-0-6453230-9-2
(Ebook)

Acknowledgements

In unity, we honour and pay our respects to the custodians of Whadjuk Noongar Boodjar country, the lands on which this book was first seeded.

We pay our respects to the Elders both past and present
and to those emerging.
The stories within these pages may contain sensitive content and/or memories of loved ones who have passed on,
which may activate a response within you.

Please read with awareness and care.

Daryl Guiver 1
Melissa Lainer 2
Joel Huey 5
Nicole Aly 8
Marilou Coombe 10
Briony J 13
Gezzell Sabina 16
Lisa Bito 19
Kate Glancey 22

Rebecca Lee 25

Emma Snelgar 30

Jenny Arnold 33

Enisa Cuturich 36

Emma Romano 39

Taryn Prince 42

Shelley Brown 45

Luzette Singh-Williams 48

Karen McDermott 51

Nicolle Weeks 53

Tanya Morriss 55

Laura Elizabeth 57

Janice Cooper 59

J.C Bell 62

ASH 66

Jess Russell 69
Ashleigh Moreland 72
Amanda Scott 75
Nina Cruz 76
Nina Cruz 80
Loving Parent 85

Daryl Quiver

Ends with Me

Just a boy with a dream to grow up like Dad,
learnt the behaviours I saw he had,
Son, don't show emotion, boys don't cry,
silence and anger are how you'll get by.
Taught me the same way he was raised himself,
as the cycle repeats itself.

Now a man with three sons growing fast,
learning to change beliefs from the past.
Strong back, soft front, stand tall and proud,
my sons can now see me, emotions allowed.
Wear your heart on your sleeve and love fiercely,
the cycle repeating, ends with me.

Melissa Lainer

All the Stars

To my gorgeous boys,

You have always been a dream of mine. Ever since I could push a doll in a pram, I have wanted the two of you. You are my dream come true, from the moment I knew you existed, now and forever.

My dreams for you are simple. Be happy. Love and be loved. Laugh, learn, and listen to your heart. Follow your dreams and know I will always be here by your side, cheering you on, supporting your next step, loving you and watching you blossom into the divine individuals you are now and will always be.

One of the greatest lessons I have learned in life that I want to pass on to you is that happiness is an inside job. It is not up to the external world or others to make you happy. You need to sit with *you* and find it within yourself. By coming home to your heart's callings time and time again, trusting your intuition, and courageously stepping forward to create the life you desire, you will find your happiness.

Along the way, others may have opinions about what they think you should be doing, but that is their business. Yours is to be true to yourself, honour your individuality, and follow your path so long as you do not harm yourself or others. It is, of course, important not to dismiss others. You can learn from them. Listen and discern for yourself whether the information others provide is for you or whether you set it free.

Letters to my Son

On your journey, you will notice that life moves in ebbs and flows. This is normal. We all feel the ups and downs, the heartbeat of life. Allow yourself to be present at each stage and in each moment. Let yourself feel. Acknowledge those feelings and find a healthy way to express and release them. When you allow your feelings to move through you, they don't get stuck and weigh you down later in life. What helps you move through your feelings will depend on the circumstances that lead to that feeling arising.

My go-to ways to move through heavier emotions are art, meditation, sound, movement, and a good old cry. Others spend time in nature, journaling, and exercising. You will need to find what works for you. I am here to hold you, listen, and help you whenever needed.

There will be constants in your life, and there will be change. This includes people, places, jobs, pets and more. These things will move in and out of your life. We never really know how long each will be around. Sometimes we choose the length of stay, and other times it is chosen for us. It is hard when things you love leave, regardless of the reason.

It can bring up feelings of abandonment, anger, sadness, disappointment, frustration, or any other feeling. At times like these, you may feel like the world is dark, that these feelings will never pass or that you have lost the light in your life, your happiness. I promise you that it will all be ok. This, too, shall pass. Breathe. Come back to your heart, and listen to what it is saying. Feel those feelings. Let them move through you and release them. It may take a while. Just take it one day at a time. Seek help if you need it, and know I am here in your heart, holding your light for you until you can do it for yourself.

Life is precious, and you are life. Take care of *you*. Find people, places, and things you love, and let them find you. Listen, learn, and explore. Discern by listening to your heart. Find your truths. Make mistakes. Learn from them. Share with others. Communicate and connect. Give from your overflowing cup. Love. Dare to dream. Find your happiness.

I'll be right there with you, always in your heart.

As I tell you at night, before you close your eyes, dream your future into being. You are kind. You are strong. You are smart, and you are important. You are gentle. You are loving, and you are generous.

I love you more than all the stars in all the skies, now and forever, your mummy. xxx

Joel Huey

Dear Son

Dear Son,

While pregnant with you, your mum asked me if I wanted a boy or a girl. For most men the answer is obvious—they always want a son. A son to kick a ball with in the backyard or join them on a fishing trip. A younger version of themselves to soak up their wisdom and share their values. But for me, I wanted daughters. I knew I could teach a son or daughter my love for cricket or gaming. But I was terrified of bringing up a son. I didn't know where to start.

When I was a boy, I knew what it was to be a man. Men were strong, brave, and independent. They were stoic and tough, gentle but resilient. But the older I got, the more confused I became. These words were jarring. I wasn't tough, and I feared leadership. I was deeply emotional but used all of my emotional energy to be in control. Other young men seemed assured about their values and ready to teach the next generation. But all I felt was a knot of fear in my stomach, and whenever I tried to confront it, tears quickly overwhelmed me. I was scared, if I had a son, I would not have the words to explain how to be a man. I didn't feel *man* enough to be a father to a son.

And fortunately, it was twelve years until you revealed yourself to me as my son. I had discovered a lot by that time and was ready to be your father.

So, here's what I know.

Men are brave and strong. But I didn't realise that true strength is discovering yourself and living as yourself. Courage is being vulnerable, especially in front of other men. Bravery is confronting your shame and overcoming it.

I thought men were independent. But the more I worked to be self-sufficient, the lonelier I felt. As I worked with more people, especially women, I learned that collaboration and mutual respect were more valuable than going it alone.

I thought men were leaders, but most men don't lead. They just follow. Real leadership is calling out misogyny and demanding better of other men. It's holding space, believing victims, and amplifying marginalised voices.

You are so lucky.

In front of you is a life of love, tears and freedom. You will surround yourself with men who cry and do not fear rebuke. They love and do it openly. They bare their soul, and are welcomed. And in this environment, you will choose to be your own man.

I grew up surrounded by caged men. The bars were built from the inside to protect me, but I was only isolated. These men worked late, drifted away, and became hidden. They were taught to be tough, angry, and never cry. When they did finally reach out, they realised they were never taught the words.

But something has changed.

Something wonderful has germinated in the emotional soil of our fathers. Gently nurtured, jealously guarded, and shamefully hidden. A desire to be more than an emotionally distant provider. While they were caged, they gave us the tools to be free. Thanks to them, we will find a place where our gender will not isolate and brutalise us and those we love. A place where we can help lift everyone.

Letters to my Son

I am forty and finally feel man enough. I am not perfect, and I constantly struggle to be vulnerable and to hold other men accountable. But I am still a work in progress. I now know that there's nothing that makes you a man beyond the way you want to define masculinity.

I choose love, vulnerability and passion. I hope you can find the words that keep you free.

Nicole Aly

The Fiercest Love

I remember how it felt to run my fingers through your hair.
To rub your back, to whisper how much I care.
I yearn to hold you, to wrap you in my arms.
To soothe your torment, to be your calm.

You seek the dark, the lonely, the hostile
Lost in the illusion, you've been here a while
One more rush, one more hit
Fast flow dopamine filling the pit

The emptiness inside you
It grows by the day
Controlling your thoughts
My son, you have lost your way

You are wild, but you are not free
Chained by your demons, can you not see
The chaos you wield, what is it you seek
Your feelings are real. Go on take a peek

Letters to my Son

Look through your eyes with compassion
See your love illuminate with your interaction
You are worthy, my son. Can't you see
You are so worthy of love, and all that can be

With total surrender, I lay down my sword
My promise to you, we fight no more
I'll never give up, nor should you
The fiercest of love I have for you

Marilou Coombe

My Darling Boys

To my darling boys,

My number one mission as your mother is to raise you to be independent, strong, yet compassionate men. I did not realise what a mission that would be when I was honoured with the task of your caretaker.

The world can be a challenging place to navigate. But, with certainty, I know you are born for these times. It is not what you do but who you are that will make a difference in the world. In your everyday actions and questions, you remind me to live in my heart space. Being a mother is not easy, but being your mother is the most rewarding role I have ever been gifted with.

I want you to remember your greatness. Of course, there will be times you won't feel so great. There will be times you will hate on yourself. But these are just moments. Don't let them be your whole life. You are greater than that!

Here are a few things I learned in my older years that I hope to teach you at an earlier age! The younger you can embody these aspects, the easier life is!

Know your values
Stick by what matters to you. I hope I can always support you with

what inspires you, even if it does not align with my values. I hope to teach you to respect yourself and what matters to you as much as respecting others. This is a fine line to tread. Just remember, when you say *yes* to someone else, you may be saying *no* to yourself. What helped me walk this line is if I say *yes* to someone else, I feel good in my body and do not take anything away from myself.

Surround yourself with the right people. Jim Rohn, a motivational speaker, famously said, 'You are the average of the five people you spend the most time with'. So, be mindful who you surround yourself with and how they influence you. Also, be mindful of your energy and the energy you take on from others.

Focus on your strengths

It is easy to get distracted by what you are not good at. Instead, shift your focus on what you are great at already and build on that. Ask your family and friends If you ever lose sight of your greatness. They will always remind you.

Take action

If you want something, make it happen. It is often said, 'Knowledge is power', when in fact, you can know *all* the things in the world, but unless you take action and go after what you want, nothing much will be achieved. Some days it may be hard, but remember you don't have to do it all in a day. Chunk it down and take small steps to reach your larger goal.

Practice mindfulness

Pay attention to your thoughts, and don't always believe what you think. You are the captain of your mind. So, cultivate it daily with positive and inspiring ideas, literature and thoughts. Mahatma Gandhi once said, 'Your thoughts become your words and actions…' they are your projection to the world. Choose them wisely and mindfully.

Be inspired

Passion only lasts so long. It is great to be passionate about things you want to achieve in life, but I have found it is better to be inspired. Being inspired lasts longer, creates better results, and most importantly, burnout won't occur. Normally when you are coming from a place of inspiration, it tends to have a long-lasting effect on the world.

Give thanks

Always practice gratitude. It is the easiest way to bring more of what you aspire to into your life. Gratitude is the highest level of frequency you can be in. So practice it often and watch how you lift yourself and those around you.

Above all, be you! You will make mistakes. You will get hurt and hurt others. You will laugh and cry, and a whole range of emotions will be felt as you grow and learn in this lifetime.

Enjoy the ride, and always know I am here for you.

Love always, Mum.

Briony J

To my Son

Dear CJ,

You came into our world bringing so much excitement, nervousness, and unknowns with all the joys and expectations of first-time parents. The busyness of parenting hit us with a shock, but your cheeky smile and happy attitude toward life was infectious. You were an absolute blessing from day one and have continued to be everyday since.

Without warning, eighteen months later, your sister passed. I was lost in the world, not knowing how to get through my grief and still be the mum you needed. I had a deluded idea of running away and leaving, hoping that somehow it would resolve my pain. But through my sorrow, I heard your cries and I knew the hard reality was not running but facing my grief.

With your innocent love and effortless ability for kindness and empathy that poured from your tiny soul, you helped guide me to the other side. You unknowingly taught me about myself, true love, kindness, and healing, and for that, I am forever thankful and eternally blessed to have you as my son.

You have made me so very proud to be called Mother. It's a name not all can receive. There may be days when you dislike my requests, rules or concerns, but it is my duty to love, care and nurture you to become the creation you were destined to be. You may question my decisions and claim over protectiveness but know that it only ever comes from a place of love compassion and fear of loss. So don't be too hard on me. I am learning everyday, and I haven't navigated parenting before. I am human, and I am trying my best. I know we both are.

My wish is to raise you to be someone you are proud of because, in the end, this is your passage, and one day when you let go of my hand and walk into the world on your own, remember that although I may not be beside you, I will never be far away.

This life we are given slips past ever so quickly, and there are no practice runs. You will have great highs and greater lows. The key is to keep going, keep getting back up—it's always too soon to quit.

Before too long, you will be a man in this world, which comes with great responsibility and countless opportunities. Society will place assumptions on you, and boundaries will be laid by your own personal integrity and beliefs.

This, my son, will be an experience of a lifetime. Embrace possibilities and build your own path. Believe in yourself, and fully live your journey by accepting your unique talents and amazing personality. Be brave enough to discover life outside society's expectations and 'social norms'.

Stand up for your values and happiness. Don't fall for the easy. Instead, fearlessly step outside your comfort zone and continue to grow. Courageously walk away from toxic circumstances, people, and relationships with respect, not hatred, and wholeheartedly embrace this existence you have been gifted.

Don't take life too seriously because we are all heading to the same place, just with different timelines. So don't be too hard on yourself or others. Remember to enjoy the small things. Take time to really appreciate the love and support around you.

Letters to my Son

Acknowledge all levels of society, remembering no one is above or below you. We are all just people trying our best in the world. No matter what others might tell themselves because they, too, walk imperfectly behind their masks. Therefore, don't allow others' opinions to fool you into a false mindset. You don't require their approval.

Keep positive, my son. This world is a crazy beautiful place where balance and love are the keys to life. See the truth in this, and the easier your path will be.

My ever-lasting words to you

Embrace your natural empathy and caring soul
Be bold, courageous and willing to learn from failure,
not petrified by perfection.
Love, kindness and justice will always set you on the right path.
You are, and will always be, enough.
You will forever have my eternal love and unconditional support.
I love you.

Love always, Mum.

Gezzell Sabina

My Mud Map

To my Beautiful Boys, Codey and Beau,

When you read and re-read this, you will have transitioned into young men, mature men, maybe fathers, and gentle-older men. Know I love you through all these transitions.

Right now, you are both so very impressionable, being so young and full of life, I'm sure it can be hard to listen to your parents. But we've been there. Things may get tough growing up. So here are some pearls of wisdom and guidance for you, my beautiful boys. I thank you for choosing me and making me your mum.

Please and thank you

These words were taught to you as a bub. This is one of the foundations of life, I believe. Asking for help and being grateful, truly grateful, will get you everywhere. All people want to feel is appreciated, you and I included. When you are truly thankful for someone's help, gesture, gift, or smile, this sits in your heart space. It will give you warm fuzzies and remind you that the simplest things in life can be the most fulfilling.

A smile costs nothing but can give so much

If dogs can sniff each other's butts as a form of interaction, isn't it a relief that we just give a simple smile?

Letters to my Son

Never underestimate the power of a smile. And you, my beautiful boys, have *amazing* smiles. The ones where your eyes disappear, and you smile with your whole face and energy. Give these freely and often. Brighten someone's day like you brighten mine.

Your word is your oath
Riches, clothes, cars, money, all the *thing*s that can come and go, but your word, my boys, your word means everything. When you speak your truth with love and honesty and from the purest part of your soul, it can't be wrong.

How other people receive your truth is not your business. They may not hear you, but they will feel your vibration. Stay true to what you say, honour what you say, follow through always. People will trust your word and choose you over and over because they'll know they can count on you. This is a blessing both to give and receive.

Don't lie, ever! It's just not worth it. If you make a mistake, own up to it. An honest mistake can be forgiven. Lies can stay forever, and you boys know right from wrong.

Listen to your body
Tune into him. This body is the only body you get this lifetime. Honour him, love him, and listen to him. Your body will let you know unseen things and feel vibrations that you can trust.

Like servicing a car, you need to take care of this body and put the right fuel in it. You wouldn't put alcohol in a nitro dragster. So don't put crap into your amazing body.

The better you take care of your health, the better your body will work for you. If it doesn't feel right, your gut will tell you. If something is off, listen to that. Once connected to the vibration of your body, the more in tune you will be in any situation.

A reason, a season, a lifetime

People and relationships will come and go. Some people will bring you the highest of highs and make you feel like you're on top of the world and couldn't possibly love or live without them. Please know you can, and you are enough.

I want you to remember these three reasons that someone will come into your world.

A reason: What can you learn? What can you teach?

A season: To teach you lessons that last as long as they are needed.

A lifetime: These are rare.

Your pop told me when I was younger, 'If you can count on one hand five people you can truly trust with your all, you are extremely lucky because most people don't get that many'.

Understanding these three beautiful-life lessons can heighten those highs and help with the lows.

I want to be the one that makes all things better for you both, that's what Mums do, but I know that if you listen and feel into that beautiful-heart space, you will remember what I have taught you and hopefully hear my voice saying, 'I love you, and you got this'.

At any time you doubt things, I want you to remember you are a part of me. You are one of only two people who have heard my heart beating from the inside.

You are all you need.

You are enough.

I'm sorry.

Please forgive me.

Thank you.

I love you.

Love and Blessings, Mum.

Lisa Bito

Growing in Awe

Dear J…,

I sit in awe of the man in front of me, the man you are becoming. So happy, independent, loving your life, spreading your wings and starting to soar. A whole lifetime of happiness and love in front of you.

But I still remember back to when you were fifteen. The year I wasn't sure you would survive.

The agony of that year still sits in my body and my heart, as I am sure it still sits in yours. However, it is lessening its grip on me, and I hope you. The happiness and ease on your face helps me with this. It helps alleviate the guilt that I failed you miserably that year, plus a few other years.

Your journey through the teenage years is challenging for me to remember. Your decision to take the hard path each time tested my strength, your father's, your sister's, others and yours. But the length of this journey was tempered by the kind-hearted, compassionate human being that shone from deep in your heart. Sometimes a bright spark, sometimes hardly a burning flicker. It is what kept hope in my heart through those years. The hope you will turn into a magnificent man and not stay an angry, tormented soul. The hope you will not choose to remain *Peter Pan* and never grow up.

I'm sorry. I stepped away. I failed you when you needed me the most. No excuses, no backstepping. I just plain and simple failed you when you needed me the most. A teenage boy was screaming without words.

It was too hard. Too much trauma and baggage of my own blocked me from seeing yours properly. Trauma created by a world that values the qualities of hate and fear over love and compassion for self and everyone else.

The pain and trauma you held in your teenage body and mind, a body and mind that couldn't and didn't know how to express itself properly. So instead, you expressed the pain and trauma the only way you knew, and the only way shown to you, through anger. So much emotion packed into your hormonal body with no healthy way to express it.

Your pain lashed out through your fists, your abusive words. A pain you couldn't understand and that I didn't and couldn't help you understand. I did not have a tool chest to help you because I couldn't see past my trauma.

They say you do the best you can with the knowledge you have at the time. Yes, that's true, but I will always regret not making a stand and finding myself and my growth earlier.

The sins of the mother revisited on the child. The guilt and anger I feel still rises. I'm not asking you for absolution or forgiveness or even understanding; I just need to tell you this so I, too, can heal. I need to face my shadow from this period in my life and ask forgiveness for myself.

I love you with all my heart, and it hurts that I added to your pain, knowingly or unknowingly.

I'm not writing this letter to make you feel guilty or ask for forgiveness. Instead, I hope it will give you some understanding of me and a way to bridge the chasm currently sitting between us.

Letters to my Son

I pray you continue to grow and the ancestral bonds of trauma continue to crumble until a man who has fully grown into his skin and power emerges. A man full of love, unafraid to show emotion. A man who is full of compassion, a man full of respect for his fellow humans, especially the women in his life. A man unafraid to show his full truth and power, a man unafraid to stand up for what he believes in, a man of integrity and awareness.

The masculine is just as damaged as the feminine. Too much pressure on being the alpha male dominates the male way through life. Forced to hide emotions and shame feelings. Forced to uphold an outdated and damaging way of being. The pressure on boys to be boys is just as real as the pressure on females to be female.

I hope you choose to sit with these thoughts and make a conscious decision to change and live a different way. I hope you choose to sit in love. I hope you choose to create meaningful relationships. Your daughters and every other female you encounter in your life will applaud you for it.

You are an amazing human, and I want you never to forget that or believe anyone who tells you otherwise. Don't ever lose that kind, caring, compassionate, empathetic side of yourself. It's a golden treasure. Let it shine out into the world.

I'm sorry
Please forgive me
Thank you
I love you.
Mum.

Kate Glancey

My Beautiful Boys

Dear Harry, Jack and Charlie,

This morning, as I sat in the silence of my new home without you here, I experienced one of the many waves of emotions that I have come to know since our family changed shape. These feelings are hard to describe and hard to put into words. They are painful emotions I have never known before.

These emotions come with all these crazy stories that I make up in my head. They are wild stories, make-believe child-like stories, arguably more entertaining than any of the action-packed *Spiderman* series where Green Goblin (me) comes to destroy the city of peace (our once happy home).

I reflected on my pain and chose to look within. What I have learned is that my pain is just that, mine.

It is not your job to fill my cup. It is not your job to heal my pain. And although Jack, you believe from the bottom of your heart and the depth of your beautiful-little soul that you truly are Spiderman with super *Spidey-sense*, it is not your job to rescue me.

I have come to learn that pain is a gift. A gift that's just as precious as that little-blue box tied with a pretty white-satin ribbon that I ask Santa for each Christmas…just maybe not as shiny or as pretty. To be honest, it usually feels more like sticking knitting needles in your eye.

But I do believe that whatever is meant for me on my journey will come to me and help me heal the pain that I hold. I believe it will help me grow. The pain I feel when I sit in the space of being without you is the greatest gift for me, for it has led me to go within myself and find what I need to feel loved, feel worthy and feel whole.

Those that say we are broken are wrong. We are not broken. You are not broken. The *perfect* life, the *perfect* family, and our *perfect* world were left behind when I learnt that the perfect mum was not who you needed me to be. I learnt that who you needed me to be, was me. I learnt that what you needed me to be was brave, real, authentic, and true. I learnt to trust that who I am, me…just me, is enough. I found myself.

I truly believe that your little souls chose me in this life for a reason. You chose me because somewhere deep inside, your beautiful, innocent, and pure souls also want to grow in this life.

When I see hurt draw tears in your eyes and feel pain flood into your heart, every part of my being wants to protect you. In some crazy-ass, mumma-bear, self-sacrificial kind of way, I think that if I just feel it all with you, then maybe I can take it away. But I know that it is not for me to rescue you either. My purpose in this life is to teach you to rescue yourself.

I will teach you to trust that whatever is meant for you will come to you and help you grow. I will teach you to trust that pain is a gift, an invitation sent from the universe offering you the chance to be brave, courageous and face your fears. I will always hold the space for you to be seen and heard, not in spite of who you are, but for everything you are.

When you find the courage to look within, you will find everything you ever need. You will find your strengths. You will see your beauty. You will know your value. You will know your worth. You will find comfort in the love of your own heart. And maybe, just maybe, you will find your very own *Spidey-sense*.

You often ask me what superpower I would choose if I could choose any superpower in the world. And even though I tell you I would choose invisibility so I can always win *hide-and-seek*, I think I may have already found my superpower.

I will always be with you on this journey. I will walk with you when you can't see the way forward. I will hold you when you can't hold yourself. I will love you so big when your heart is open, and I will love you even bigger when your heart is closed. And when you find yourself lost, I will guide you back to yourself.

To have loved you every day of your life, held you in my arms, and nurtured your precious hearts has been the easiest part of the privilege of being your mum. I know in my heart that you know you are loved. The greatest gift I can offer you is to show you how to love yourself.

So, I guess what Peter Parker's Uncle Ben said really is true, 'With great power comes great responsibility'.

Love, Mum.

Rebecca Lee

Poems for my Son

His Fray of Depression

The battle of night does not unravel at dawn
He always awakes weathered and worn

Within unconscious fray, he sits motionless
A devil on each shoulder

Begging for the abrade of disdain
Rotted sour eats away

In violent pain, a temper flares with no cooling
Throes of strain remain

Struggle as he might to find the light
His angels rest out of sight

Reapers Torment

Your blind eyes turn away from the wasteland
Letting retched souls sink or swim

Every soul carries their darkness
A bitter seat within

Do you disconnect from every source to keep the demons at bay?
The stench of your ignorance is where I see the reapers torment lay.

Letters to my Son

Gather the Souls

To stars, we shift our heavy sigh
Extend to night a fateful goodbye

Clouded dreams, in a trance, we sway
Boundless time in which we lay

Gather together the souls at rest
Earthbound journeys faithful test

Sever the scar but not the tie
Bless the beauty as it hides

Beneath the tear is breath of life
Sheltered heavy, and fearfully tight

Hold the thought, steady the hand
Your heart is heavy but memories grand

Deep Dive

Past a glistened shore
beyond rockpool welts
of superficial shredding

a tumble and polish by ebb and flow
wave after wave on crashing
this skin shivers

submerging relentlessly
bruised and battered
by the masses of undercurrent

I see clearly the ocean floor
hinging my precipice

and I deep dive
not to drown, but to survive.

Taking Flight

I reign the sky, both day and night
A bird of prey taking flight

I am wind-driven
Weightless and rising above cumulus formation

Eloquently soaring the northerlies
Freedom amidst no earth-bound land

Ruffled feathers gifted by plight

Wings span wide

I roam the sky in darkness and light

With eagle eyes and falcon sight.

Emma Snelgar

I Love you

To my two favourite boys,

There are some things I want you to know about this world.

In our previous generations, the onus was on the child to make the parent proud. Parenting was very behaviourist in that the child was seen as an extension of the parent. Thus the parent was judged for the behaviour of the child, resulting in all sorts of issues for that generation.

My generation is one of cycle breakers who see the child as a whole human with their full spectrum of needs and emotions, all of which are valid and welcome. Parenting against the grain and meeting you where you are at, mothering you in a way that respects and honours you, whilst holding huge boundaries against the generation above us, has been a lot of work. The generations above us, who judge us for being too soft, for *'creating a rod for our own back'*, who want us to *'toughen you up'* have not always understood our reasons for parenting in such a conscious way. And I haven't always gotten it right.

So instead of wanting you to make me proud, I hope that I have made you proud. Because we need to keep looking forward, and you are going to inherit this world that we are continuously co-creating.

But in saying that, here are some gentle reminders.

Firstly, please know that to make mistakes is to be human. I am not perfect, and I don't expect you to be either. Make as many mistakes as you need because, as you know, making mistakes is how we learn. Give yourselves the grace to allow the mistakes, apologise when you need to, and take the time to appreciate and integrate the lesson. This is growth.

Secondly, your sensitivity is your superpower. If something feels wrong, it is. I love how you are not afraid to call people out who are rude to you. As you grow and expand your awareness to those around you, continue to use your voice and speak up for yourself and others. Even if you need to call out a friend for poor behaviour, do it, but do it with love. Also, on that sensitivity, keep feeling and showing your emotions. We are at a pivotal time where we are shaking off the culture of toxic masculinity and patriarchal control. Recognising and feeling your emotions is a sign of strength, not weakness.

And thirdly, as you continue to grow, self-responsibility is where it's at. You are responsible for your own health, environment, and how you are feeling. No one can make you do or feel anything that you are not in agreement with, and you always have the power to change what is not working for your highest good. This is why I go on about looking after your own things and picking up after yourself, because learning self-responsibility starts at home, of course!

I hope when you grow up, the world has changed for the better, and I don't need to remind you of this, but I will say this anyway. If you choose to have a family, support the mother of your children, assuming you partner with a woman…you are only six and eight. Share the mental load. Make sure she is not always the only one reaching out for help and support in the community, and make sure that she is not the only one having to think of what is for dinner every night!

Lastly, I want to thank you both. Thank you for choosing me to be your mother. You have been my biggest teacher and the biggest catalyst for personal growth and expansion. You have filled my days with such overwhelming pure joy and love, and I love watching you grow more and more into yourselves every day.

I love your confidence, your kindness and your loving hearts. If I can offer one more thing, you are both perfect just as you are. And if you both grow up loving who you are, I will consider my job to be well done. For two little rods in my back, you've done alright so far… wink wink!

I am eternally grateful that I got to be your mother in this lifetime. And in our next lifetime, we already have plans to be together again.

Felix, if you read this when you're older, and you don't remember this—you want to come back as my cat. I am to call you *Fluffnugget*, and you don't want to wear a collar.

Ollie, you just want to be a human boy again.

I love you both,

always and forever,

Mum.

Jenny Arnold

Sunshine through my Window

I know it's cheesy, but the day you were born was the best day of my life. It was the first day I'd felt true love. The first day I felt whole. The first day I felt nothing else mattered. You came to save me from the depths of my inner despairs and past traumas, from the inner turmoil that haunted me daily. You came to me at the perfect time in my life. You literally were the sunshine through my window.

The day you were born was a long day. You were so comfortable there, and nothing worked to get me into labour. I knew you wouldn't come the conventional way, and after a long nineteen hours, you were born by caesarean section. I was exhausted! You were such an angel because you let me have time to recover, only waking for food and a hug with a tiny whimper. You were such a calm baby.

I'm sorry the relationship with your father didn't last. I did everything I could. These things happen in life, and it didn't bother me being a single parent. Our relationship grew even stronger. I made sure you had everything you needed, which was love and protection. I tried to make sure you had a relationship with your father and Grandma, seeing them as much as possible, they did love you just as much, and it worked.

I then had a new relationship with your stepfather. We really wanted to have you grow up in a loving family unit because we didn't have that in our lives. Your sister was born when you were three and a half years old. You loved her instantly and became a proud big brother. You both became best mates and had so much fun growing up. We all went on awesome family camping trips. I wanted the best for you both.

When you were eleven, we decided, as a family, to move to Australia. You were so keen to go. Even though you knew you were moving away from your father and Grandma, you already had a strong instinct that it was meant to be. A new life in a country where you could grow up instead of our hometown, with lots of crime, a scary place for you as a child. You felt it wasn't safe to play outside.

Growing up, during your teenage years, you suffered from anxiety. Like most teenagers, hormones ran riot, but your stepfather always seemed too hard on you. You felt you were treated differently from your sister, and I just wanted to love and protect you. Those were my instincts, and I never wanted him to upset you in any way. Yes, I felt so much guilt and despair for you. But sometimes, teenagers need that strictness to guide and build them up. And you needed it, even though you couldn't see that at the time. You did not realise it, but we loved you no matter what.

Today, you are independent, work full-time, and have your own place, too far from me. I feel the separation every day, even though we talk every day. I know you are making your own life, and I must let you be free.

You have become an amazing man with a huge heart. You are so grounded and confident, even though you would disagree. You know what you want and don't want. I love that we have a close relationship, and you seek my guidance when you need it. The relationships we have all together are unique.

Letters to my Son

We have always been honest with each other. That is our superpower. I am so extremely proud of you, and my heart bursts with joy and love for you. I cannot wait for the day you have your own family. The girl who wins your heart will be so lucky because of the true gentlemen you have become. Do not change for anyone, Son.

You are amazing as you are, and I love you to the moon and back.

Eniza Cuturich

My Luka

'This little Luka of mine, I am going to let him shine…' I've sung this to you every day since the day you were born.

My heart skipped a beat when they told me I would have a son. I was both so beyond excited but also terrified.

All the men in my life were nothing like you. They had already made their choices, decided who they were, and weren't open to change and what it meant to be a man.

You, my Son, were so different. When I looked into your eyes for the first time, I knew that you were a part of something so much greater. A leader in the next generation of men who will redefine and embody what it means to be the king of his world.

There are a lot of distorted views of what it means to be a man and a lot of really soul-destroying expectations, which has a lot to do with the men on the planet abandoning themselves, numbing their feelings and taking their pain out in toxic ways.

The men I grew up around, my dad, Granddad, uncles, and great-granddad, were all this way. They were all abused by their families, wives, alcohol, drugs, money and themselves.

There were never taught how to be the king of their world, to love themselves, love others, face life challenges, talk about their fears, feelings and desires and hold space to listen to others.

All those things were taught as signs of weakness to them.

I never had a solid role model for what it meant to be a man. My dad abandoned me when I was seven years old, and all the other men that came into my life after that weren't great examples either.

Until I started to learn who I was, heal from trauma and choose to take full responsibility for my life, aka become the queen of my world, was when I started seeing kings all around me.

I saw men who followed their passion, shared their hearts and were willing to take responsibility for themselves and their behaviours and heal from whatever trauma and shame they held.

I started seeing men who were present with their kids, loved their wives, were willing to work on their relationships, and always chose to do and be their best.

These kings were showing up for themselves, their family, their friends, their businesses, and their lives. They were great examples for me to redefine my own meaning of *man*.

It was foreign to me and broke my heart because I wished my dad was like that or had been open to discovering himself.

It took me twenty-seven years to understand that my dad's actions were not a reflection of me, meaning it was not because I wasn't lovable, a good daughter, enough, worthy or deserving.

He was in a lot of pain and held a lot of past trauma, which kept building and building every time he would get abusive, drink and avoid facing it all.

The lesson is that your parents, family, friends, environment, and anything external to you, do not define you. Only you can define yourself. You are the king who gets to create and lead his kingdom however he wishes.

As your mama, I believe it is my role to create a safe space for you to discover who you are, to love and support you, to guide you and lead by example, showing you that following your heart and doing what lights you up in life will create an extraordinary reality.

You are so powerful, so capable and will be able to create whatever life you wish to have.

My promise to you is to share the wisdom, tools and opportunities to support you in discovering and mastering who you are. Building an *unfuckable* relationship with yourself because no matter what anyone says, including me, yes, I know I'm putting this in writing, but you are the only person you have to love unconditionally. As life happens for you, understand that you are the creator of your vision, and there will be people who tell you that you can't, say *no* or put doubt in your mind.

But that is *why*! You *must* master, love, accept and build an unshakable relationship with yourself.

I also promise you that I will *always* be here for you, no matter what. I will love you unconditionally, be your safe haven, do my best to be a healthy and limitless role model, be the best Mama I know how to be, allow you to be one hundred per cent you, and never give up on you in any way!

You are the light of my life and the biggest gift I have ever been given.

I love you.

Emma Romano

My Young Men

My sons,

My young men. My muse's. Thank you for teaching me how to be the best version of myself. For wanting better and being better. Thank you for your endless love, patience and kindness.

My letter to you holds so much love, excitement, and wonder. Love for the young men you are in all your ways. Excitement for the journey you are on in all its ways. And wonder in how you choose life and what you do with it.

I want to put something in this book that I know I have told you, but I want you to pick this book up and read this any time, at any age and at any experience you are going through.

If something feels right, do it. If something feels wrong, get out of agreement with it. Move on. You have *everything* within you already to feel worthy and amazing. You were born with the birthright of this. Claim it, own it, live it and be it, my Darling Hearts.

My advice to you is this. There is only one thing you really need to be in tune with, and that is this, agreement. So what are you in agreement with? Are you in agreement with fear? This will only stop you from living your life to the fullest, darling hearts, and get you to half-arse life.

Or, are you in agreement with inspiration? This will find you in a place of excitement and adventures, and in this space, you will notice that there are *no* mistakes, only opportunities to learn and grow and find who you truly are.

It's your choice.

It's always your choice.

Be loyal to your values and morals, not to negative relationships and situations. You don't owe anyone anything, only yourself. Do life with great kindness and compassion. Understanding someone's pain and reactions are far more powerful than making yourself right.

Choose your fights. But always fight for yourself.

There are two ways you can be a man. You can be a prince and feel the world owes you, or you can be a king and create the world you imagine.

I'm not sure if you know this or not, but you are truly magnificent. You have journeyed through many lifetimes, and this journey with me has been beautiful, difficult, loving, fun, and challenging with so much love and deep, deep conversations.

I have your back. I will always have your back.

You are so deeply loved. Read that again. *You are so deeply loved.* Breathe that in and see where in your body that hits you. That is love, Darlings. That is *love*.

Anything that you do, give it a red hot go. Be enthusiastic about it, and create excitement around it. Produce your own high frequency into it and just see the abundance flow in.

Everything is energy, my Darlings. You know this. What you put in, you get out. So if life is shit, it's because that's what your frequency is running at, and that's the agreement you have created. Change it. It takes seconds. Stand up, shake it off, call your mother, hug the dog, crank up some tunes and go outside and move. Know that I love you deeply and am here for you to rest on.

Letters to my Son

Family and this Universe deeply support you.

I love being your mum. It's my favourite thing in the world. You are a blessing to this Universe. Thank you for coming through me. I honour you. I love you.

You already have everything inside of you to be happy. Enjoy the journey, Darling Hearts.

Love you.

Love, Mummy.

Taryn Prince

My Beautiful Boys

To my husband's one

I'm sorry you had to find out at eleven years old that your dad was not your biological parent
I'm sorry if you felt lied to
I'm sorry that we weren't given the opportunity to tell you
I'm sorry if you have ever felt abandoned by us
I'm sorry if you've felt lost
I'm sorry we've missed out on so much
I'm sorry if you don't know how much we miss you
I'm sorry you have never met your brothers
I'm sorry if our love has never been enough
I'm sorry that you are now grown and have no need for us…we still need you

To my number one

I'm sorry that your conception was overshadowed by the loss your dad felt for his first boy
I'm sorry that I cursed you, curled up alone on the floor, with severe morning sickness

Letters to my Son

I'm sorry that your birth was so traumatic that I couldn't hold you, or bond with you
I'm sorry that you were a week old and you fell off the bed
I'm sorry I took unsolicited advice and lacked the knowledge to breastfeed you longer
I'm sorry that you were born with severe allergies
I'm sorry I didn't understand you were in pain all those sleepless nights
I'm sorry you scratched and scratched and bled constantly, and I couldn't make it better
I'm sorry for all the hospital admissions in those first years
I'm sorry that your dad had long, long, swings at work

To my missed one

I'm sorry if I wasn't sure if I wanted another baby. It was too soon
I'm sorry I didn't look after myself better and nurture you in the first few weeks
I'm sorry that I lost you, a loss no one should ever experience

To my number two

I'm sorry I was scared and stressed about losing you
I'm sorry I spent sleepless nights in the hospital with your brother while growing you
I'm sorry that I pushed so hard for the perfect birth and again was met with trauma
I'm sorry your daddy had to go back to work when you were only one week old
I'm sorry I couldn't handle two under two, solo, for weeks on end
I'm sorry that I had to drive round and round to get you both to sleep

I'm sorry that my attention was sometimes pulled in all directions with your brother's medical issues
I'm sorry for waking to your cries only to realise I was asleep in your brother's bed
I'm sorry I then resorted to co-sleeping to ensure we all slept and knew where we all were
I'm sorry I sometimes feel so touched out that I can't hug you

To both of you

I'm sorry that you are now four and five, and I'm trying to wean you both from co-sleeping
I'm sorry I get so overwhelmed and stressed
I'm sorry that I often can't control my anger
I'm sorry that it's just the three of us the majority of the time
I'm sorry I cry…a lot
I'm sorry I'm so shit at cooking dinner
I'm sorry we are isolated logistically from your beautiful extended family
I'm sorry I'm free-range
I'm sorry I sleep in, and you make your own breakfast
I'm sorry I can't give you everything you want

To all of you

I'm sorry I didn't make more of you
I'm sorry that I love you all so much it hurts 'infinity one hundred' and more than the 'university'

Love, your mumma and your stepmum. xoxo

Shelley Brown

All my Love

Dear K,

The way you came into the world was not as I envisioned. I was lost when I couldn't hold you as soon as I woke. The nurses held a picture in front of my face. I couldn't focus. It could have been a photo of any baby. How could it be my baby when I wasn't conscious for your arrival? Even when I saw you and held you, I was scared I'd break you...in all the ways. I worried we wouldn't bond after lost, early moments. I was concerned my anxieties would become yours—you may not have dodged that particular bullet! Then to have your long-awaited sister be a bit complex and take so much of my time seemed a heavy load for one so little.

I think back to the little-blonde boy who gladly had chicken nuggets delivered to his darkened, *PlayStation*-equipped cave and was perfectly happy. Most content to race cars and shoot baddies in your own company or that of a close friend.

But you have pushed yourself and surpassed your comfortable place. You found the strength to strive for yourself. Not everyone can do that. You did. You do. There need not be a constant push to deserve accolades. Steady steps, when you can, have walked you all the way here. I see you now with a clear focus. My baby boy is a delightful man.

I have my idea of what a good life looks like for you. Not that it's my business, but I'll tell you anyway. My hope for you is happiness. A life mainly feeling content. With a purposeful role. Friendship to make you smile and keep you balanced. Spirituality in whatever form that takes for you. A full belly and a warm place to sleep. Curiosity about the world to widen your horizons. And, something I know I can tick the box on is that you eat your green vegetables. Oh, what a proud moment it was for me when you first ate broccoli without gagging.

I am sorry for some of the difficulties you have experienced. No eight, nine, or ten-year-old should have to help time a seizure and clear the doorway for paramedics. Nor should any kid hear a suction unit fire up, knowing it would be a difficult day.

I am sorry for the pain and worry. I cannot know the lessons in these experiences for you, but I hope you see them. The darkest moments allow wisdom to illuminate. You have much light to share. I know you wouldn't wish for a different life if that meant a different sister, but I will never know just what this life has been like through your lens. Like me, I hope you feel grateful for the lessons, love, and laughs along the way. I hope the adoration on your sister's face when she looks at you outweighs the times she has scared us all.

You are an extraordinary human. This isn't news to me. The level of compassion, insight and intellect you hold is beyond measure. The way you think is amazing! Pre-parenting theories would have me believe my job was to impart all my wisdom and give you the tools for life. How arrogant of me to think I was that important.

All the million-little decisions you made, your interests, the people you connect and surround yourself with, what to focus on, and what to let go of are all you. *All you*!

Whatever choices for the tools you needed, you made. Whatever influence I thought I might have, the light that shines, that's you—an extraordinary human.

I smile, thinking of you, your kindness, empathy, humour and joy. There is a reason for you to be resentful. I could understand why you might be scarred. Yet you rise. The heights you are reaching are lofty and so well deserved. Enjoy this view of life, my love. You have worked for it.

You made me a mum, and you have taught me so much.

I came across these beautiful words from eleven-year-old you, 'I love my life. And I love you, Mum. You are the topping on my ice-cream!'

And you, my gorgeous one, are my sprinkles!

Thank you for being you.

All my love, Mum.

Luzette Singh-Williams
To my Boys

'I'm not saying I'm going to change the world, but I guarantee I will spark the brain that will change the world. That's our job—to spark somebody else watching us.' -Tupac Shakur.

Lights! Camera! Action! The world is filled with roles that we adapt and mould ourselves to fit in through the different facets of life. The roles we adopt, portray, and sometimes suppress, make up who we are when we find our place in the world. Through growth, we are often like a plastic bag in the wind, pulled in different directions by societies 'yes, no, stop, more, not like this and not like that'.

What I offer you is a suggestion of how to be so still and grounded that, like a beautiful tree, only your leaves move and change with the seasons. Yet, your trunk and roots stay strong, and connected to something else that brings you peace. It is a place that cannot be touched, moulded or influenced unless it is for your greatest good.

Many amazing guides have written the guidebook to life, yet there is no set way to live for every person. You need to recognise that your growth is constantly evolving and what worked today may not work tomorrow. What I offer you is to look to nature and the elements to connect you to a place of peace.

Letters to my Son

Air: New Life Communication Power of the mind
Earth: Abundance Solid foundation Nurturing fertility
Water: Subconscious Purification Psychic
Fire: Creation Destruction Re-creation

In every living human are the elements reflected in nature. Therefore, the structure under which the masculine living in this world is constructed often goes against what you feel. Your role isn't necessarily what you have been shaped to believe, so in order to break free from *The Matrix*, nature will offer you a beautiful reprieve.

Why? Because throughout humankind's history, mother nature has always stood strong as a neutral space for stillness. Feel the energy of nature and your ancestors. Feel into your inner being, and know yourself first without conforming to labels to know what feels right.

Sounds tricky? It is, and yet it is so simple. I invite you to strip away all labels and don't ask who you are. Instead, feel who you are. When you connect to your body, to the present moment, you will receive the answers to what you are made up of.

Our wonderful men, placed upon this earth as protectors, are often pushed into a world of violence, possession, gritting and bearing teeth. This path always leads to internal and external destruction, so we must simply stop and re-assess. Using your gut feeling and intuition as your internal compass will always be your strongest guide.

Dig deeper to source peace and joy. What a beautiful gift to share with others and to know this feeling within yourself without external conditions.

Peace and Joy? Is that it? Yes, it is.

These are two powerful forms of energy to help you to strive forward. When you feel peace, competition, jealousy, anger, envy, and depression aren't present. You just are. Fear, despair, pain and sorrow no longer have a place when you feel joy. Instead, you will see joy and opportunity in everything you do, good or bad.

When we take life's events and view them through a lens of joy and peace, we strip away labels and what remains is the essence of human nature. Ask yourself, does this action or thought disrupt my peace and joy? If it does, change it, amend it to be more aligned with who you are and what supports your growth.

YOUR growth never stops, so don't feel that you should conform to certain stereotypes, and be prepared to trigger people when you don't conform to certain ways of being. That's not your concern. Just stay the course.

FEEL all your emotions. Each one holds messages for you. Never be afraid of them, but don't allow them to consume you, be in them, feel them, hear the message, and move forward.

Often the male species is frowned upon for listening to emotions and allowing them to guide you. But I promise that your emotions hold their weight in gold. So collect these golden moments, and they will help you stay grounded and understand life as it unfolds.

SEEK information. Never stop learning. A job or role does not mean you are set. It means you have a role to play at this moment. But remember, the role of a student lasts a lifetime. Never be afraid to change if it feels right to you.

Dedicated to Ruka and Shaan.

Love, Mum.

Karen McDermott

Love Life

To my sons,

You may have been born ten years apart, but the love you receive from Mum is unconditional and the same.

You were born into two different environments and were born to two different Dads, but one thing you both share is the heart of a mum who will love you unconditionally and forever. Please learn from this, and allow yourself the grace to live from your heart.

I have discovered, in life, that not everyone has been blessed with unconditional love. My hope is that you identify and value this gift I have given you so that it helps keep your heart strong in times of need.

My advice to you is to do life your way and prioritise joy and love intently!

You may be of Irish heritage, but please don't fall into the trap of being the macho male who is just a hunter-gatherer. It is important to have a beautiful life balance of providing but also to claim your position in the family as an equal caregiver. We all need to allow love to flow through and from us to feel the benefits of being truly alive.

Treat them with respect, and allow their growth when you are blessed with a life partner. Support them, but also ensure you receive the same in return. Truly value love and work hard to maintain it.

Know relationships have ebbs and flows, but there is always something to build on if the essence of love is there from both people.

And if you choose to learn to love unconditionally, it will ripple through to future generations and make a real difference. Know that you are loved and use that love as a catalyst to pursue your dreams, to have the courage to make them happen. Please take some time in your life to answer the call to learn my universal teachings. They are not gobbledygook. You have watched first-hand and absorbed the process by being around me during the process, and if I can do it, so can you. But the main thing is to do it for you, not me.

Really know what it is you want from life. Don't let anyone tell you. You are the only one who knows exactly what you want. Avoid later regrets by honouring your dreams now, and grow into the person you need to be to receive them as the next natural step.

Please have the courage to stand up for injustice in the world but know that it doesn't have to be through hate. You can make a difference by speaking up and supporting those in need, and quite often, the perpetrator is the one who needs to know what it is like to be a good person so let them experience that without you being taken advantage of. A beautiful balance is to be had when you do it with a more open mind. Know that everything can be remedied when it's done with loving attention.

I hope you carry my words in your heart and that others feel their benefits too. Please know the power of love in our personal and professional lives, and our world needs more of it, especially from our boys.

Love life, and it'll love you back.

I love you both.

Nicolle Weeks

Special Moments

You are the one who blessed me with the privilege of motherhood and kept me grounded as I stumbled my way through those first few years—those first few years when it was just the two of us for months at a time while your dad was away working.

I often wondered how I would make it through the day. All of a sudden, I was alone with this little baby. I didn't know what I was doing. I was so young and so utterly naive about the pressures of this new life. But you gave me a purpose! The deep, unshakable feeling of love and wholeness that I had never known drove me to want to be the best version of myself for you.

These first few years feel like they have flown by. But at the same time, it feels like we have been together for an eternity. I am sure only a moment ago, a tiny baby lay where now a boy sleeps—my boy, my silly, loving, kind, free-spirited boy. This life with you is everything I dreamed of and a million times more. I am your safe place, and you are mine!

I soak in this time with you as we prepare for your baby sister to arrive. You look up at me and kiss my pregnant belly as curiosity fills your thoughts, and you ask me a million questions about your growing little sister. You are so full of excitement and wonder about our next new journey together, you as a doting big brother and me as the proudest mother of two. I wouldn't want to share these moments with anyone but you!

You are nine now. Where has the time gone? I often reflect on those early years, and tears fill my eyes as I long for the baby that you once were. I miss that baby! Transitioning into your pre-teens, we begin another dive into the unknown. My hope for this next stage of our life together is that a new closeness blossoms between us. It will be different than it was before, but we are different. I feel such a deep need to keep you as my little boy forever, but I also feel excitement for what the future has in store for you.

I understand you are beginning to figure out who you are and who you want to be, and I have noticed you are beginning to see the world differently than you once did. I'll admit sometimes I'm just a little jealous because now it's all about Dad! But, I watch on lovingly as the two of you share your little inside jokes, your special father and son bond reserved for just the two of you. I feel so very out of the loop but so completely at peace.

We still share our own special little moments. From time to time, you pass by me in the kitchen and wrap your arms tightly around my waist for no reason at all. Then, in the most genuine and affectionate way, you tell me that you love me, and I feel loved! No one can make the world's pressures melt away quite like you do when we share those special moments.

When one day a man stands where my boy once did, these are the memories my mind will wander to. I will remember the little moments we shared, and I hope you know you have been so unconditionally loved when you look back on your life!

Love always, Mum.

Tanya Morriss

World of Difference

My boy,

You are my beautiful, sensitive, strong and honest-little man.

Entering this world, I gave you my all. The feeling of empowerment you gave me was unlike anything I had or will ever experience. Your addition to our little family made me feel so proud. Georgina has a little brother! Your daddy now had a little girl and boy to love and protect. Such a big change from the life we knew, and so very welcomed.

Watching you grow from a baby into a little man has been a world of privilege. You feel everything with your heart. A strong warrior, like your daddy, is deep inside. There will be times in your life when you will need to call upon this strength to get you through. This will be your journey to make. I know with all my heart that you will light that fire within and face whatever challenge comes your way.

If there is one lesson I have learnt, it's that life is all about timing. Every choice you make will lead you to the next until you end up where you are supposed to be. Moments will happen in your life that you will not see coming. Some will bring copious amounts of happiness, and some will bring pain you never thought possible. We just have to ride the wave until the sea calms. It always does. Even if it feels like you're drowning, it will always come to settle.

My eyes are open to the person you will become, and I wonder what kind of difference you will make in this world. The difference you have made in my world is indescribable. My mum used to say once you have kids, it's like a revolving door. I was so young and never really understood what she meant by this. My interpretation of what she meant, is that your children come back to you at different times in their lives. Know that I will always be there for you when you come back around every time.

I hope for nothing more than a smile that cannot be wiped off your face and copious amounts of joy in your life. This is all of what you deserve and more, my little ray of sunshine.

Laura Elizabeth

Showing me Love

I know love is real because you both exist.

Before I became a mother, I foolishly believed that raising sons would be a breeze compared to raising daughters.

But the truth is, there is so much out there to help scaffold and nurture your sister through life. There are books, resources, and sister circles aplenty designed to sculpt, hold and raise the next generations of empowered women.

But what about our men?

Who is speaking up on behalf of you?

Sure, there are men's gatherings and influencers talking the talk, but it still feels like we have to dig deeper. It still feels taboo for men to be conscious, grounded, centred as well as brave and stoic.

As soon as I held you in my arms, Cooper, I knew I had a duty and responsibility to guide you on a path that nurtured your sensitive heart, as well as your practical mind, and make it normal.

To raise you and your brother as two solid examples of what it means to be a whole man. To celebrate your feelings and your strength and teach you to have compassion for each other and those around you.

At just twelve years old, already taller and more intelligent than your mother, I can already see what an incredible young man you are growing up to be. Honest and responsible, caring, and strong. You have never been afraid to feel. This one truth makes me so proud of you every day.

Ewan, when you completed our family four years later, with your sister in the middle, it was like you had been here forever.

You have such strong intuition that enables you to instantly disperse uncomfortable energies and moments in a room. You are unafraid to be the one standing up and stirring things up so that everyone feels safe and relaxed. Your ability to bring fun into every moment makes us all want to soak up your sparkle.

My boys, thank you!

Thank you for leading the next generation of men. Thank you for being brave enough to show that you care, feel and love. Thank you for carrying the heavy bags from the car. Thank you for being the most perfect examples of centred, healthy masculine no matter what you are faced with.

And most of all, thank you for showing me real love.

I am proud of you, and I love you beyond.

Love, your mum. x

Janice Cooper

Completion of our Family

Dear David,

I write this chapter to convey what it meant to have you complete our family unit.

You were a much longed-for second child for us. We had our share of heartbreak along the way, with a miscarriage in July 1990 and a scare in my pregnancy with you in February 1991, when we thought we might lose you too. Your birth was pretty intense but extremely quick, and we were both relieved and overjoyed that you arrived safely.

You grew so fast, and as you developed, so did your quirky little personality, which showed me that you were no *ordinary* child. You were always happiest when within reach of me, and such a stickler for routine, we had a very special bond from day one.

Knowing you would be my last baby, I admit to possibly being a little overprotective of you, which may have held you back a little.

As a toddler, you became proficient at imitating cartoon characters and friends who visited. With extreme attention to detail, you would copy, and you had an awesome sense of humour even at a very young age. You were painfully shy and introverted with strangers, but doing your *impersonations* or dressing up as a superhero, you forgot your shyness, taking on the make-believe persona.

You disliked change, so our move to Australia from Scotland when you were seven was a huge challenge for you. You struggled at school, mainly because you didn't conform to the school environment, but you did what you could, and you tried hard.

Very intelligent, but not applying yourself was the common saying amongst teachers throughout your schooling. But a breakthrough came when you were invited to join the music program in year six. You decided you'd like to learn guitar.

The music program was a pivotal and defining time for you that led to a more confident and happier personality shining through. You excelled in your guitar lessons and practised for hours, proving to me that you were dedicated to improving your musical knowledge.

You began to write songs, and by the early days of high school, you could always be found in the music room, either in your class or *helping* the music teacher with other students.

Lots of concerts and performances followed at school and at weekends, and you were clearly happiest when on a stage performing in front of whatever gathering was there to watch you. It didn't matter whether there were five people or fifty people, you were just happy to play and sing. From being a shy, awkward little boy, your passion for music allowed you to express yourself in ways you otherwise wouldn't, and you became more confident.

One of my most precious memories was your year seven graduation. You were chosen to play the lead character, Jimmy, in the production, and you absolutely shone that night. We were all so proud of what you'd achieved. After the performance, there were so many parents who paid tribute to the great job you did, and most were stunned that the shy young boy from the classroom had just *wowed* the audience.

I have so many memories of school concerts, gigs with your mates, practising in the garage on weekends, and trying to think up original band names. Now, at thirty years old, you have such a vast knowledge of all things pertaining to music, and now you teach and share your skills, helping budding musicians.

It wasn't always easy steering you in the right direction, my son. School was extremely frustrating for both of us at times, and I often worried that you'd be left behind.

Thankfully, you have grown into one of the most respectful and caring men I know. You rarely judge others and always try to see the good in everyone. Your trusting nature has sometimes led to you being hurt emotionally, but this adds to your resilience, makes you stronger, and creates great songwriting opportunities.

I hope this chapter is something you can look back on with fond memories of me when I'm no longer around to ask you lots of questions when you come over for a visit. In writing this, I intend to make you aware of how much your presence in our family enriches my life in ways I never thought possible when I held you for the first time.

David, I am so proud to call you my son and so happy you chose to join our family. Never change. Keep being the beautiful soul that you are. You are so much to so many.

Love you always,
Mum.

JCBell

The Narrative

Being a mother wasn't something I thought about. Mainly because I believed I'd be terrible at it. The idea was ridiculous at best and horrifying at worst, considering my hectic-drug fueled lifestyle. Being told it was either impossible or a complete no-go early in life put babies out of my mind.

However, the 'no baby for you' information didn't compute until I finally settled down and could get pregnant, and my body viewed the little things as foreign. Like any 'country' invaded, my uterus waged war. I lost many and, with them, any hope. So, you can imagine my shock when I got pregnant, and the baby made it past eight weeks and then past twelve. But now, the real fear kicked in. Not fear of having a baby, but what if that baby was a girl?

Honestly, the thought of having girls frightened the shit out of me. I didn't feel equipped for that. Before we understand that we can change the narrative, break the cycle, we are products of our environment. And while my father was great, he was absent, and the industry I entered when I was seventeen was thick with men who took what they wanted and used their fists to solve their problems. They stalked their worlds and ruled with archaic-neanderthal brutishness that was toxic masculinity at its finest.

I've thought about why I wanted to write for *Letters to my Son* when

Letters to my Son

I don't have a son, and the answer, after some deliberation, was because it was time to understand why I was so scared of having girls.

I always thought it was because I was scared that the things that happened to me would happen to them, and I would be powerless to stop them. I was terrified their voice and body would be marginalised. I think somewhere deep down, I thought I could teach a son not to use their hands in anger. I could teach him to be kind, thoughtful, respectful, loving, strong, fearless, accountable and brave. I could teach him it's okay to feel emotions and express them with tears and sadness.

But I was blessed with three little girls instead of the boy I thought would suit me. Three little girls that I can teach how to stand up for themselves. Three little girls that I can teach to question societal normalisation toward women and men. I can teach three girls to be kind, thoughtful, respectful, loving, strong, fearless, accountable and brave.

Even though I don't have boys, I realise I still have something to offer the world's males. So while I will teach my girls to be fearless and stand up for their rights, I will also teach them not to adhere to stereotypes and societal expectations of what 'masculine' means or what 'feminine' means.

I think, well, I hope, as a society, we are moving toward a greater grasp of what it means to not only minimalise the voices of women but always the hearts of men.

We genders inhabited traits throughout history relegated to one gender or the other, and these traits defined us. These ideologies shaped society even though we all know women can encapsulate great strength and men are capable of great depths of feeling. One, or the other, doesn't define hardness or weakness. Definitions of 'gender' can be movable, fluid and indefinable.

I hope going forward, for the sake of men and women, that meaning surrounding historical engendered ideologies of 'maleness' and 'femaleness' continue to be questioned and continue to evolve.

My hope for the future of men is that we allow little boys to cry, express their emotions and talk about their feelings, wear pink or love romantic movies and not be ridiculed as soft.

I hear parents of boys say, 'Well, boys will be boys,' when their sons do things stereotypically deemed 'boy' behaviour but are wrong regardless of gender. This saying makes me sad because we are choosing to perpetuate the male myth that aggression is masculine. I've heard parents be disappointed when their son doesn't stick up for themselves by using violence to retaliate against bullies. Instead, they are made to feel weak. What is that saying about the definitions we place on our children?

I hope we teach boys not to use their hands in anger but instead to channel pain and rage into something that allows them to release energy without causing more despair. I hope that boys are shown by the men in their lives that control is better. I hope these boys turn into men who treat their daughters the way they want other men to treat them. Listen to your daughters, don't dismiss their feelings as dramatic, and don't dismiss their emotions. Be empathic and kind. I hope that boys are shown a different understanding of what it means to be a man, and in turn, they become men who allow their sons to be more than a stereotype.

So, here is my advice as a mother of daughters and ultimately a mother of humans.

Pay attention. Pay attention not only to what you need but also to what others need around you. If you end up marrying a woman, pay attention. If you end up marrying a man, do the same.

If you have daughters play tea parties with them. Lay with them

Letters to my Son

at night and read to them. Let them paint your nails and dress you in pink. Show them a dichotomy of meaning. Show them that a man can be soft and strong, and show them that they can be too. Teach them to be strong and fierce and how to change a tyre and light a fire. Show them how to love by showing them love and acceptance. And if you have sons, do the same.

If you choose a path where you don't marry or have children, live your life respecting others, male or female.

Don't be undone by men stuck in centuries of defunct meaning.

Stand up, even if sometimes you stand alone.

Listen to your friends when they are low. Be there, really be there. Let your actions reflect your words. Pay attention to the people around you if you see deep silence or you see them fall. Be there to help them stand.

Be brave

Be strong

Be fearless

Be kind

Be understanding

Be emotional…

Be more than what has come before.

Change the narrative, and those around you will be grateful.

ASH

Warriors of Love

I'm Sorry

Please Forgive Me

Thank You

I Love You

I am sorry for the untamed emotions you have witnessed. I was yet to feel safe with the wild and chaotic parts within—a space of chaos and confusion. The moments when I felt alone and scared and turned to you for understanding, support even. These were not your responsibilities to hold.

I'm Sorry

Please forgive me, as I am learning to forgive myself. Please forgive yourself for anything you think you may have done. You are my hero—hear my praise, please forgive me? As I am learning to do. It was a time for discovery and learning, raising you, my sons. Although my intentions always come from love, I also often need forgiveness.

What is *right* for me, is not always *right* for you. For this, I pray you can remember that I am human, dancing within polarities until the pendulum finds its centre.

I am but a simple human, experiencing this crazy life with no instruction manual.

Please Forgive Me

I have done the best I can, with the resources I had, in each and every moment of raising you, my sons.

I strive every day to love you in ways you need to be loved.

Talk To Me

I Miss You

Thank you for your love and your teachings in raising and understanding the male species. I know now that I have a lot to acknowledge. Misunderstandings, I assume, because we are made of different stardust.

Venus and Mars, I have heard…

Thank you for awakening me to the challenges of growing into a man in this modern world.

Where are your Warriors?

The Initiators?

Where are your Guides and credible Elders?

Please know I am seeking. My greatest wish is to cross paths with men who are courageously stepping into elder roles—open hearts and vulnerable in their truths and capacity to give and receive love.

Creating that safe container for you to fully feel all you are.

I Love You with every essence of my being. And yet, as you become older, I am struggling to connect. I know independence needs to occur, and I miss my little boy.

I Love You, and I want you to know that I see how hard it is for you.

In the depths of your being, may you always know that my love for you is as expansive as the Milky Way, the type of love that will drive a person insane should they become too attached. For this is your path to walk, your lessons to be learned…

I love You, and I hope you know you can come to me with anything.

May you find ways to choose Power over Force.

May you remember your Power stems from within.

ASH

May you know *Power* is *Life-Giving*, whilst *force* is *life depleting*.
With Power comes Oneness
Unity
My Warriors of Love, how proud I am of *You*.
Love, Mum. xo

Jess Russell

My Love

Connor, my heart, my mirror, my teacher, my inspiration.

From the moment you were conceived, everything I ever hoped for and wanted in life changed. I could no longer hide from my own shadows and fears. And from that moment forward, everything has been about being the best version of myself that I knew how to be because it was no longer just about me and my life. I wanted more. For myself, for my family, and for every generation that follows.

I spent years trying to work through all the trauma and emotional disconnection I experienced growing up. All of the things I never wanted you ever to feel or experience yourself.

I will always do everything in my power to make sure you feel seen, heard, and, most of all, loved.

I know I can't protect you from everything, no matter how much I want to.

What I can do is, teach you what I know.

Nothing in life will ever be perfect because nothing and no one on this Earth is! *We're* not meant to be! You just have to find your own version of what's perfect for you.

We're meant to make mistakes! How else will we learn what we are truly searching for in this life? We have to figure out what we don't want, right?

Life is about showing up! And never giving up, no matter how hard things may seem.

There are so many lessons throughout life, and there will always be challenges, no matter how old you are. The trick to surviving the ups and downs of life is to feel it and live it!

Face each moment head-on and listen to what your gut is telling you. You've been here before, my darling, and you have all the answers. They are all there, deep within you. Trust your instincts, and always listen to that inner voice. And although life can be hard at times, and things may not always go as you hoped or dreamed, we have to keep going!

We all have a purpose and a reason for being on this Earth, at this moment, in this time! We each have a special gift that we are here to share with the world.

We spend so much of our lives trying to please others before we finally realise we must put ourselves first.

When you finally decide to do all those things that make you come alive with joy, things that set your soul on fire, that make you feel like you finally know where you belong, then you will know what true happiness is because you will know yourself.

You don't need others to tell you that you are enough or to tell you who and what you should be in *your life*! You know who you are, and I hope that you can see just how amazing you are already.

No matter what life throws at you, keep the fire in you alive, and never let anything or anyone take it from you.

You have so much passion and wisdom inside of you, and your imagination is truly limitless! I watch as you take on the world and absorb it all. Your ability to imagine is beyond anything I've ever known. You see things in so many different forms, and to you, nothing is impossible.

Letters to my Son

I see more of you than I could ever explain.

Watching you grow up is like watching a piece of my heart and my soul right there in front of me.

I know that the world can be hard, and I can feel you struggle with it all.

Take it all in. Feel every emotion and moment of joy and happiness, as well as the pain, the hurt and the anger.

We are all born with a loving heart and divine soul. And through life and experiences, we change, and sometimes we close ourselves off.

I know that I will not always understand what you're going through, but I am always here, and I will always try and help you through whatever you're going through in the best way I can.

Some days that help will not be what you want or expect, but I hope that you know that everything I do, is to help you learn and grow in this world. To help you become the most amazing version of yourself possible!

So every day, I pray for you to hold love in your heart and light in your soul.

You are one of the kindest humans I have ever known. And I can't wait to see you grow and change the world. Because I know that you can! And you will, my love, you will.

Ashleigh Moreland

Infinity and Beyond

Lijey Lou, I love you.

When you entered this world, you altered my life forever in the absolute best way imaginable. You gave me the gift of motherhood. You accelerated my trajectory towards growth unlike any other experience or interaction in my entire life. You exposed my blind spots, awoke the fierce advocate in me, and taught me about unconditional love.

Lijey, as I write this, you are almost nine years old. You love *Pokémon*, maths, gaming, reading and skateboarding. Sometimes you feel like you don't fit in, or you are different. The truth is, you *don't* fit in, and you *are* different. I didn't fit in either, and I was different too, and it took me far too many years to realise that standing out is our gift. It is our blessing.

Lijey, you have a way of seeing the world that most don't understand. You have a way of *feeling* the world that most don't understand. I pray that as the world shakes you, shifts you, squeezes you and pulls you trying to mould you to be just like 'the rest', you lean into God. And be filled with the strength and knowledge that you are *exactly* who you were born to be, *exactly* as you are in this very moment.

Right now, you are entering a phase in your life where you have heightened awareness of worldly constructs, and you are exposed to adult concepts that are a giant leap from your childlike innocence. As your mum, my instinct is to step in and protect you. I want to shelter you from the hurtful words or actions of others, but my soul knows that to know love, we must experience hurt. To know joy, we must experience sadness. To know faith, we must experience fear. I know that if I shelter you, it comes from my selfish need to control your 'okay-ness', and it disempowers you from your journey of growth. However, I promise I will always be your safe place, honour your heart and soul with the highest regard, and give you unconditional love.

I pray that the eyes of your heart remain open and that you can express love, compassion and grace towards others if they are projecting their pain or fear onto you through unkind words, actions or behaviours. I pray that you can have such a strong sense of self that it feels safe for others to journey home to their 'selves', too.

Lijey, I couldn't be prouder of the person that you are. You will make some big mistakes and many small ones, but always remember that *you* are not your mistakes and that mistakes are always a learning opportunity. Your past is the past, and each moment is a new opportunity for a fresh start.

If there were any wisdom that I could arm you with, it would be to be aware of fear. Fear is a foothold to steal, kill and destroy, and it will strip you of all kinds of opportunities, connections, relationships and significance if you don't claim victory over it.

Don't let the fear of getting hurt by people steal, kill and destroy your ability to love and trust. If you are hurt three times, learn from it and love four. If you are hurt thirty times, learn and love thirty-one. True, authentic love is the greatest gift of all.

Don't let the fear of failure steal, kill and destroy your pursuit of the things that set your soul on fire. If you try, there is a small chance you will fail and not achieve what you want. If you don't try, there is a one hundred per cent chance you won't achieve what you want. It is safe to try, and it is safe to fail because every failure is an opportunity to refine and try again.

Don't let the fear of rejection or judgement steal, kill and destroy your willingness to show up as your authentic self. The world needs your light. If you don't express it in fear of what others think, you will contribute to darkness by depriving others of your light. Have gratitude for rejections or negative judgement, as they're not aligned with your path. Show up with integrity, love and grace, and this will be your non-stick coating.

Lijey, there are so many other fears you may face in your life, too many for me to outline here, but any time you're conflicted, ask yourself if this is of love or fear, and is it life-giving or life-taking?

I love you to infinity and beyond, always and forever,
Mum.

Amanda Scott

Love Always

To my growing son,

I am your number one supporter, but I hope you have many.

I have your back, and I want the very best for you.

When I ask, 'What are your goals?'
I mean, what are you planning with your health?
What are you doing to connect with your friends and family?
What are you planning for fun?
How are you setting up your environment and room for best energy use?
How are you giving back? Donating clothes, or doing something like putting a trolley back for someone without them knowing.
How are you going to keep a positive mindset?

How are you feeling?

Good?

Love always and forever, Mum.

Nina Cruz

Greatness in You

You came into the world with an unstoppable nature and made me a mama eleven years ago. A precious and priceless gift bestowed on me. A gift that keeps on giving. Giving to me in so many beautiful and true ways. You became my teacher. Teaching me so many powerful lessons, some lessons harder than others some days, and boy, how naïve of me to think I would be teaching you!

How grateful I am you chose me to be your mama.

You arrived with a bursting spirit for life, action-packed, wild and free ready to explore and conquer the world. Who was I to try and hold you back? I learnt that you were little Mr Independent 'all by myself Mama'. If it wasn't nailed down, it was going to be moved! Some things never change. Your deep sense of knowing exactly what you desired meant I needed to be on my game. I needed to find my own sweet spot between holding you and letting you go.

You've shown me how to be present and reminded me not to 'sweat the small stuff' and to have fun and play. 'Other things can wait, Mama! Let's grab our capes and be superheroes! Let's fly through the sky on our next adventure together!'

You're strong and courageous, so I had to parent outside the box, follow your lead and be curious at each stop. I realised early on that your big ideas and plans were always better in your hands.

Letters to my Son

You reminded me of so many beautiful truths. That Mother Earth is more important than the prime minister, and Aboriginal and Torres Strait Islander peoples are the original land owners. I felt you as you spoke about what was deep within your heart. You feel it deeply. You showed me how to look after all creatures, great and small. So much wisdom, my little-old soul.

You are a force to be reckoned with. As your teacher said, 'A freak of nature'. You shine at anything you focus and put your mind to. Gentle but strong, firm but kind, sporty and athletic—you're always throwing a ball around the place. I learnt many *ninja-like* skills to duck and weave the throw and be nimble on my toes. I admire your love of baseball and the joy it brings me to watch you play passionately on the field.

So, my beautiful boy, I want to remind you of some ancient truths so you continue to remember who you truly are.

You are a powerful creator
There is nothing you need to fix or change about yourself. All you need to do is love all the parts that make you, *you*. From the strong warrior that lives within, to your loving and kind-compassionate soul. Embrace those parts that feel because they reveal your tender heart, the most powerful part of you. Love even the parts that feel unlovable. They all add up to you.

Revel in your freedom
No shoes, no rules, and keep your curious spirit alive. Run like the wind and set sail to all the dreams brewing inside, ready to take flight in the world. You are the magician. Your creative genius lives within you. So follow your heart and do what you love. Bring into being your

great imaginings because if you can dream it, you can have it. There are no limitations, only the ones you put on you.

You are the wizard that creates in your mind first

Nothing can stand in your way when you are focused and hold that vision. Your imagination is the gateway—so dream big, my little one. Let no one or no thing stand in the way of your mission here on Mother Earth. You are the longing of life itself.

Plant the seeds you desire to create in your mind, nourish them, and nurture them into fruition. And remember, just because you can't see it with your two eyes doesn't mean it's not happening. So many wonderful things are bubbling away under the surface, ready to be fully expressed in the world.

Hold the vision that your desires are coming and will burst through into the light. Just like a seed sprouts a tiny shoot that leans toward the sunlight, keep faith and trust.

Have patience, my dear one. I know it's hard. I feel your restlessness, but be one with the resistance. Welcome it because what you resist persists! And from this place of surrender, your creations will come into form. You will magnetise them into being.

Be authentically, unapologetically, divinely you

Be the very thing you desire to create and have. Don't mould or contort yourself to fit in. Just be you! Stand up, carve out your own path, and follow what feels right. When someone isn't so kind, and it hurts, remember their pain, see beyond what's happened and be the bigger person.

You are the magic.
You are the creator.
It's all inside of you.

Letters to my Son

Don't search for something outside because it's all within. Just unwrap all the magic that lives inside of you.

Remember, greatness lives inside of you. You carry it wherever you go. A butterfly doesn't question they can fly, so trust in you, then spread your wings and fly. Fly high above the sky, and I will be there by your side to watch you soar above the clouds and in the abundant blue sky.

Nina Cruz

Poems for my Son

Bittersweet

Time goes by.
You grow before my eyes.
I try to cling,
to stay here forever.
But as the winter snap comes
without warning,
you to change.

Bittersweet

Emotions swirl
as parts of me hold on
because the letting go of you
is the hardest part of it all.

I want to stay suspended in time.
In a bubble with you in your childhood days,
singing, dancing, playing and laughing,
in awe of you.

Letters to my Son

Words can't express these feelings,
the blessing you are to me and the world.
Fly high sweet one,
I can't contain you, nor can anyone.
My memories of days gone by living sacredly in my heart.

So I watch from afar a little more.
My love is always connected to you
by an invisible string,
with you even when we are apart.
And I'm ready when you call for me.

I thank the stars, the moon, the sun
for gracing me with your presence.
For the gift of you.
Can't hold the longing for life back,
Cannot remain the same,
it must be set free.

Spirit soaring high,
way beyond the clouds.
I acknowledge and hold those tender parts in me.
They long for you to stay in the bliss of this moment,
with me,
and never grow old.

As night turns to day,
and darkness turns to light,
I couldn't ever hold you back.
As time moves on,

Nina Cruz

harsh yet majestic,
you can't hold back a rain cloud,
nor hold a raindrop in your hand.

Slowly it slips away,
falls back to Mother Earth.
To its original belonging,
it's custodian of life.

Bittersweet

Untethered and wild,
I watch with amazement,
my heart sings with joy
for the blessing and grief I can feel at times
on this journey of mothering you.

Let me be your Safety

Let me be your safety
from the storm
Let me tend to your needs
Let us snuggle so tight
that you feel my presence
Let it melt away your fears
and put at bay your tears

Let me be your shelter
from the storm

Let time slow down
so you can feel my love
that it penetrates all worries and concerns

Let me be your safety
your blanket
that holds you safe and secure
when life feels unsure

Let my love emanate all around you
swallow you up
so you know what it feels like
to be loved forevermore

Nina Cruz

Let me be your safe haven
when things feel overwhelming
Let's breathe through it together
as we breathe the same air

Let me be your signpost
to remind you of your greatness
when you feel small and unsure

Let me be a mirror to you
the precious gift that you are
that was bestowed upon *mi amor*

Let's dance together
and play this glorious game
For when we can soften the hard edges of life
we can see obstacles becoming
bridges to our soul

Let me be your shelter, my dear one
May you rest in me
May you know the profound depth
my heart feels for you, sweet one
And may this safety and love help guide you on your way beyond all storms.

Loving Parent
A Letter to your Son

Loving Parent

Letters to my Son

www.ingramcontent.com/pod-product-compliance
Lightning Source LLC
Chambersburg PA
CBHW020328010526
44107CB00054B/2024